MAKE, BAKE, CUPCAKE

tips for top cupcakes

MAKE, BAKE, CUPCAKE

tips for top cupcakes

This edition published by Parragon Books Ltd in 2014
LOVE FOOD is an imprint of Parragon Books Ltd

Parragon Books Ltd
Chartist House
15–17 Trim Street
Bath BA1 1HA, UK
www.parragon.com/lovefood

ISBN 978-1-4723-3001-7

Printed in China

New text and editing by Anne Sheasby
Designed by Talking Design
Illustrations by Charlotte Farmer

Notes for the Reader

This book uses both metric and imperial measurements. Follow the same units of
measurement throughout; do not mix metric and imperial. All spoon measurements are
level: teaspoons are assumed to be 5 ml, and tablespoons are assumed to be 15 ml. Unless
otherwise stated, milk is assumed to be full fat, eggs and individual vegetables are medium,
and pepper is freshly ground black pepper. Unless otherwise stated, all root vegetables
should be peeled prior to using.

Garnishes, decorations and serving suggestions are all optional and not necessarily
included in the recipe ingredients or method. The times given are an approximate guide
only. Preparation times differ according to the techniques used by different people and the
cooking times may also vary from those given. Optional ingredients, variations or serving
suggestions have not been included in the time calculations.

Contents

Chapter 1:
On Your Marks, Get Set!

Setting up before you begin

- Make sure your work surface is clean and dry and clear of anything that you don't need when preparing your cupcake recipe.

- Be organized and check that you have everything you require to make, bake, decorate and serve your cupcakes. Gather together all the ingredients you'll need and set out the equipment required within easy reach, before you begin.

Reading the recipe before you start

- It is important to take the time to read through the entire recipe, from beginning to end, before you begin to make sure you have all the ingredients and understand the directions.

- Check to see if any part of the recipe needs to be prepared in advance. For example, soaking dried fruit in fruit juice before adding to the cupcake batter or making chocolate ganache in advance to give it time to cool and thicken before use, and so on.

- Check that the total number of cupcakes the recipe makes suits your requirements. If not, consider whether the recipe is suitable for halving or doubling the quantities given.

- Check that you have the necessary basic equipment to make the recipe. If the recipe calls for any specialist tools or equipment, check that these are essential to use (before you purchase them) or if you can substitute with something similar you already have.

Assemble all the ingredients and make sure that you have enough of each ingredient – you don't want to have to dash out for another egg halfway through the recipe! Butter or margarine and eggs should be at room temperature. The butter should be of a soft, spreadable consistency.

Take time to carefully weigh out and prepare (where necessary) all the ingredients before you begin to make your cupcakes. Accurate preparation of ingredients, especially in baking recipes, is vital for successful results.

Essential ingredients – choosing

Whatever cupcakes you choose to bake, the finest quality ingredients will always give the best flavour. Here's a guide to some of the basics you'll need.

Butter or margarine (or alternatives) – Butter (unsalted or lightly salted) or soft tub margarine can be used to make cupcakes, although butter will give a richer and creamier flavour. Hard margarine can be used but its flavour is inferior and you won't get the same rich buttery taste.

Low-fat spreads are not usually suitable for baking, as they contain a high proportion of water.

Flavourless white vegetable fat or shortening, which is suitable for vegetarians and vegans, can be used as an alternative to butter or margarine in some recipes.

Whichever you choose (but particularly so with butter), remove it from the refrigerator at least 1 hour before starting to bake and leave it at room temperature, as it needs to be soft all the way through to be successfully creamed with the sugar.

For the best flavour, use unsalted butter for delicately flavoured cupcakes, buttercream icings and frostings.

Oil is occasionally used in cupcakes, such as carrot cupcakes, and will produce moist cakes. Use a mild flavoured oil, such as sunflower oil.

🧁 **Sugars, syrups and honey** – Caster sugar is ideal for baking as its fine grains dissolve easily, making it ideal to cream smoothly with softened butter or margarine.

Other sugars, such as soft light and dark brown sugars, have more depth of flavour than white sugars and add richness and colour to your cupcakes. If possible, choose unrefined or muscovado brown sugars which have an excellent flavour.

Demerara sugar has large golden crystals, which add crunch and texture when sprinkled over the tops of cupcakes before baking.

Icing sugar has a fine powdery texture that dissolves easily, making it perfect for buttercream, royal and glacé icings and frostings.

Golden syrup, maple syrup and honey are all useful sweet syrups to keep in the storecupboard. They can be used in place of sugar in some cupcake recipes or for frostings and glazes.

🧁 **Eggs** – For the best baking results, always use fresh eggs at room temperature. If eggs are too cold, they will curdle the creamed butter and sugar mixture. Be sure to use the correct egg size for the recipe – the recipe or cookbook should give guidance on the size of eggs required.

- **Flour** – Cupcake recipes either use self-raising flour or a combination of plain flour and baking powder or bicarbonate of soda. Always check that self-raising flour has not passed its best before date, as the raising agent will be less effective. To make your own self-raising flour, add 2 level teaspoons of baking powder to each 225 g/ 8 oz of plain white flour.

To incorporate as much air and lightness into the cupcake batter as possible, sift the flour before using. If using wholemeal flour, remember to tip any bran left in the sieve into the mixing bowl, as this is the most nutritious and flavoursome part.

- **Raising agents** – Both baking powder and bicarbonate of soda are used as raising agents to produce light and airy cupcakes. Baking powder is a mixture of cream of tartar and bicarbonate of soda.

Only buy these raising agents in small quantities and check the best before date before using as they have a limited shelf-life.

- **Flavouring extracts** – Vanilla and almond extracts, when used sparingly, can add a wealth of flavour to a simple cupcake batter and other natural extracts, such as lemon, orange and peppermint, are also available. Be sure to buy natural extracts, not synthetic flavourings (essences).

For delicately scented cupcakes, invest in a small bottle of rosewater and orange flower water.

- **Cocoa powder** – Cocoa powder is a fine, reddy-brown powder that has a bitter but intense chocolate flavour. Unsweetened cocoa powder is widely used as a flavouring in cupcakes, other cakes, bakes and desserts. It can also be lightly sifted over baked cupcakes as a decoration.

Essential ingredients - weighing

🧁 Make sure your scales are positioned on a level surface and weigh out all ingredients before you start to mix.

🧁 It is important to make sure that all ingredients are carefully weighed and measured. Accurate measuring is critical to baking and the success of your recipe will depend on it. Too much or too little of any one ingredient and you will have less than perfect results.

🧁 Use measuring spoons where possible, especially for raising agents and flavourings.

Top tip
It is much more accurate to use a measuring spoon, rather than a kitchen spoon.

Essential equipment - selecting equipment

The beauty of baking cupcakes is that you really don't need a lot of expensive or fancy equipment. Most of you will have the few necessary basics in your kitchen already. However, some specialist items are worthwhile investments, making techniques easier and improving your skills. Cake decorating shops and good kitchenware stores are useful sources, or check out the many suppliers online. It is also worth buying good quality equipment that will last a long time – if you regularly bake cupcakes then invest in a good bun tin. Here's a list of the basic equipment you'll need to get started.

Kitchen scales – Accurate measuring of ingredients is a major key to all successful baking, so a good quality set of scales is essential. Digital scales are the most accurate and some have a useful add-on facility that allows you to re-set the display to zero and weigh out another ingredient on top. Cheaper spring or balance scales are just as good if used correctly. It's essential to always follow either metric or imperial measurements for a recipe – not a mixture of both. If you use digital scales, keep a spare battery handy.

Measuring spoons – Using a set of standard measuring spoons will ensure that small quantities of ingredients, such as baking powder, vanilla extract, ground spices or other flavourings, are measured accurately. Measuring spoons are usually sold in sets of 4, 5 or 6 spoons and will measure out between ¼ teaspoon and 1 tablespoon. Always use a level spoonful, unless stated otherwise in the recipe.

Measuring jug – A heatproof glass jug or a transparent, hard-wearing plastic jug with clear markings on the side will make measuring liquids easy. Choose one with a good pouring lip and clear markings, either metric or imperial.

Mixing bowls – Although you only need a large mixing bowl for making most cupcakes, it's useful to have a selection of 2 or 3 different-sized bowls, so an assortment of sizes is ideal. Toughened and heatproof glass bowls are hard-wearing and practical. Melamine or ceramic bowls are available in a variety of colours and look attractive in the kitchen!

Sieves – To sift dry ingredients and remove any lumps, you will need a large (rustproof) metal or nylon/plastic sieve with medium to fine mesh and a set of three sizes is useful. A small, fine sieve or tea strainer is also handy for decorating cupcakes with a dusting of cocoa powder or icing sugar. After washing metal sieves, make sure they are thoroughly dry before putting away.

Spoons – You'll need wooden spoons for creaming and mixing, and a metal spoon for folding in ingredients. Wooden spoons are cheap to buy so it's worth having a few in a range of sizes. Always make sure they are dried thoroughly after washing and throw away any that are old or split. A good-sized metal spoon is essential for the folding-in stage of cupcake making. Heat-resistant nylon, silicone or melamine spoons are durable and less flavour-absorbent and can be used instead of wooden spoons.

Electric mixer – Although not essential, an electric mixer makes light work of mixing cupcake batters, icings and frostings. Hand-held ones are easy to manage or a freestanding mixer is useful for many mixtures. The same results can be achieved by beating with a wooden spoon or balloon whisk but it will take longer.

Spatulas – A flexible rubber, silicone or plastic spatula is useful for light mixing of ingredients and scraping down the mixture from the sides of bowls. A spatula with a spoon-shaped tip is ideal for scooping up mixture to fill cupcake cases and piping bags.

Bun/muffin tins – To ensure even cooking and a good shape, cupcakes are best baked in metal or silicone bun or muffin tins/trays. They usually have 6 or 12 holes to sit paper cases in. Some metal tins have a non-stick coating, which is useful if you want to make cupcakes without paper cases. Reusable, flexible non-stick silicone bun/muffin trays come in a variety of bright colours or pastel shades and can also be used without paper cases.

Bun tins usually have fairly shallow holes with gently sloping sides whereas muffin tins have much deeper holes with straighter sides. The type of tin you use will affect

the appearance of your cupcakes – for a slightly flatter and wider cupcake use a bun tin and for deeper cupcakes with straight sides use a muffin tin.

To make mini cupcakes, you'll need a mini muffin tin. These usually have 12 or 24 holes.

Wire cooling racks – Once baked, cupcakes need to be transferred to a wire cooling rack to allow them to cool quickly and evenly. If you plan to make batches of cupcakes, it would be useful to invest in a tiered wire rack, which will save on worktop space.

Box grater or flat grater – A hard-wearing, stainless steel box grater or a flat grater with a firm grip handle, are good for grating citrus rind, apples, chocolate, nutmeg, etc. It's useful to have a fine, medium and coarse grater.

Citrus squeezer/reamer – A sturdy plastic, metal, toughened glass or ceramic squeezer is used for extracting juice from citrus fruits for adding to cupcake batters, glazes, icings or frostings. A wooden or plastic reamer squeezes out the juice by simply pushing into the halved fruit, but you may also get some pips.

Essential equipment - choosing cupcake cases

Paper baking cases make cupcakes look appealing and they also make them more manageable and easier to transport. You'll find a huge range of paper baking cases available in shops and online. Paper cases are usually greaseproof so they generally do not need greasing before use. As a general guide, there are 4 sizes of cases:

- Muffin cases – large deep cases with straight sides, these are perfect for making big American-style cupcakes.
- Medium-sized cases – these are similar in size to muffin cases, but tend to have narrower bases and hold a little less cupcake batter.
- Fairy cake/bun cases – shallow cases that produce small English-style fairy cakes or cupcakes.
- Mini muffin cases – ideal for bite-sized mini cupcakes.

Silicone cases are a fantastic modern invention and are available in a range of colours, sizes and novelty designs. Most stand up by themselves so you won't need a muffin or bun tin – just pop them on a baking sheet. The main advantage of using these is that they are reusable.

Whatever size of baking case you use, remember not to over-fill them and adjust the cooking time accordingly.

Patterned paper cupcake cases – These are widely available in numerous different colours, patterns and sizes, including themed, contemporary, vintage and children's cupcake cases. Mini baking cases are also available, if you are baking mini cupcakes.

🧁 **Paper-lined foil cupcake cases** – These are also widely available in different colours, patterns and designs. Mini paper-lined foil baking cases are also obtainable.

🧁 **Shaped cupcake cases** – For something a bit different, shaped cupcake cases in standard and mini sizes are available and include scalloped, petal, floral, tulip and ruffled-style cupcake cases. You can also buy reusable non-stick silicone cupcake cases or cupcake baking cups in standard and varying novelty shapes, as well as plain or pleated paper baking cups.

Preheating the oven

🧁 Ovens can vary considerably, depending on whether they are gas, electric or fan-assisted, so always use the oven temperature in the recipe as a guide. If your oven runs a little hot or cold then adjust the temperature accordingly. Fan ovens tend to be hotter and cook more quickly than conventional ovens, so reduce the temperature by 10-20°C/50-68°F or follow the manufacturer's recommendations. An oven thermometer is useful for checking the accuracy of your oven.

🧁 Always preheat the oven before you start baking (check the recipe to see at what stage you need to do this). Preheat the oven to the required temperature for 10-15 minutes before use, so that it has time to reach the correct temperature.

Greasing and lining cupcake tins

🧁 Always follow the recipe instructions about preparing tins.

🧁 With most cupcake recipes, you will line the bun/muffin tins with paper cupcake cases, so there is no need to grease the tins before use.

🧁 If, however, you are not using paper cupcake cases (perhaps you would like smooth-sided cupcakes instead of pleated ones, for a change), grease bun/muffin tins with melted or softened butter (preferably unsalted) or a flavourless vegetable oil. Spray vegetable oils are also useful for greasing tins. Alternatively, a bun/muffin tin can be greased and floured before use.

🧁 Using a piece of kitchen paper, you can wipe a thin film of sunflower or vegetable oil over the top of the bun/muffin tin, before lining the holes with paper cases, if you like. If the cupcakes then rise above their cases during baking, the greased surface will help to prevent the tops of the cupcakes sticking to the tin.

Chapter 2:
Let's Get It Started!

Basic recipe for vanilla cupcakes

Makes 12
Preparation time: 10 minutes
Cooking time: 15–20 minutes

115 g/4 oz butter, softened, or soft margarine
115 g/4 oz caster sugar
2 eggs, lightly beaten
1 tsp vanilla extract
115 g/4 oz self-raising flour
1 tbsp milk

1. Preheat the oven to 180°C/350°F/Gas Mark 4. Line a 12-hole cupcake or bun tin with paper cases.

2. Put the butter and caster sugar in a large bowl. Using a wooden spoon or an electric mixer, beat together until the mixture is pale, light and fluffy.

3. Gradually beat in the eggs. Add about 1 tablespoonful at a time and beat thoroughly after each addition. Beat in the vanilla extract.

4. Using a large metal sieve, sift the flour into the bowl. Using a metal spoon, gently fold the flour into the mixture until thoroughly incorporated.

5. Add the milk and fold gently into the batter. The cupcake batter should have a smooth consistency and drop easily from the spoon if tapped on the side of the bowl.

6. Carefully spoon the batter into the paper cases, dividing it evenly and taking care not to over-fill them.

7. Bake in the preheated oven for 15–20 minutes, until the cupcakes are risen, golden and just firm to the touch.

8. Leave the cupcakes in the tin for 5–10 minutes, then carefully transfer to a wire cooling rack. Leave to cool completely.

Flavour variations for the basic vanilla cupcakes recipe
- Lemon or orange – omit the vanilla extract and add the finely grated rind of 1 small lemon or orange to the butter and sugar in step 2.
- Chocolate – replace 2 tablespoons of the self-raising flour with cocoa powder.
- Coffee – replace the milk with 1 tablespoon of cold strong black brewed coffee.
- Almond – replace the vanilla extract with 1 teaspoon of almond extract.
- Peppermint – replace the vanilla extract with 1 teaspoon of peppermint extract.

Basic techniques

🧁 **Creaming** – Butter or margarine and sugar are beaten together thoroughly to form a light, pale and fluffy mixture. It's essential that the butter or margarine is a soft, spreadable consistency before you start – but not melted. Use a wooden spoon or an electric mixer on a low speed and take care not to over-beat or the mixture will become oily. This will take at least 5 minutes by hand or 3–4 minutes with an electric mixer.

🧁 **Separating and adding eggs** – To separate eggs, tap the shell against the side of a mixing bowl to crack, then break open, letting the white run out into the bowl and holding the yolk in one half of the shell. Carefully tip the yolk backwards and forwards from shell to shell to let all the white run into the bowl.

Always beat whole eggs before gradually adding them to the creamed mixture. Add the beaten eggs to the creamed mixture about 1 tablespoonful at a time. Beat well after each addition to make sure all the egg has been incorporated before adding the next spoonful. If the mixture begins to curdle, add a couple of spoonfuls of the measured flour before adding more eggs.

It's best to use eggs at room temperature for baking as they give a better volume and hold more air when whisked. If you usually store your eggs in the refrigerator, remove them at least 30 minutes before you start to mix.

🧁 **Adding flour and folding in** – Always sift the flour with any raising agents or spices before adding to a mixture so that they are evenly distributed.

When folding in flour or dry ingredients, use a large metal spoon to gently cut and fold them through the creamed mixture with a light, quick action to keep as much air in the mixture as possible. Make sure to scoop up all of the mixture from the bottom of the bowl.

Don't over-mix when folding in the dry ingredients. Over-mixing can knock air out of the batter and result in heavy, close-textured cupcakes. Don't use a wooden spoon or beat the batter as this will also knock out air bubbles and produce close-textured cupcakes.

🧁 **All-in-one method** – This is a simplified variation of the creaming method. All the ingredients are beaten together at once until smooth. If you follow the all-in-one method, the recipe will call for a little extra raising agent (baking powder) to compensate for the air not being incorporated during the initial creaming stage. This extra baking powder helps to make the cupcakes rise and soft margarine or butter is essential for it to mix fully. This method gives close-textured cupcakes and is an ideal method when you are short of time.

You'll need to use an electric mixer for the all-in-one method and take care only to beat enough to combine all the ingredients to a smooth and creamy batter.

Whisking – To make whisked egg white-based frostings (or meringue-type toppings), large amounts of air need to be incorporated and trapped into the whites. For speed, use an electric whisk or use a large balloon whisk and lots of elbow grease!

With egg white-based frostings or meringue-type toppings for cupcakes, the egg whites and sugar are whisked together until the mixture is thick enough to hold stiff peaks. Egg whites at room temperature will whisk better than cold egg whites, so make sure you take eggs out of the refrigerator at least 30 minutes before you use them. Also, use fresh eggs that are only a few days old to get the best volume.

Getting creative with food colourings and surprise fillings!

Adding food colourings – Food colourings are available in a variety of colours in either paste, liquid or gel form. Pastes and gels give a good deep colour and are best for colouring cupcake batters, marzipan, fondant icing and royal icing. Liquid colourings can be used for colouring cupcake batters, glacé icing, buttercream and other frostings.

When adding food colourings, always use a measuring spoon (or sometimes the bottle may have a drop dispenser, especially useful with liquid colourings) and don't measure the colouring directly over the bowl of batter or icing, just in case of a mishap. Add the colouring gradually and in small amounts and mix it in thoroughly after each addition until you achieve the desired depth of colour.

🧁 **Adding surprise fillings before baking** – For extra appeal and variety, you can add surprise fillings to your cupcakes. The surprise filling is baked within the cupcake batter, so that when you bite or cut into the cupcake, a surprise is revealed! The filling can vary from baked cake shapes (such as a heart or teddy bear) to mini brownies, pies, biscuits or cheesecakes, or shop-bought sweets or chocolate.

Top tip

A small piece of chocolate makes a great surprise filling for any chocolate cupcake.

To insert a filling into cupcake batter, simply spoon a generous tablespoon of cupcake batter into a paper case, then place the filling, such as a cake shape, upright in the middle or position a brownie or other item in the middle, then spoon more cupcake batter around the shape or around and over the item, filling the case about two-thirds full in total. Repeat with the remaining cupcake batter and filling items. The cake shapes won't be fully covered with batter but the smaller items such as mini brownies and pies will be fully covered by the cupcake batter. Bake, cool, decorate and enjoy your filled cupcakes!

🧁 **Layered or marbled cupcakes** – Another way to add flavour and interest to cupcakes is to make layered or marbled cupcakes. Layered cupcakes are made by piping different coloured cupcake batters into paper cases in flat layers, one on top of the other (to make rainbow-style cupcakes). You can also add a different flavour to each or several of the coloured layers before using, if you like.

Using two different coloured batters, you can also create diagonally layered cupcakes and marbled cupcakes.

Diagonally layered cupcakes can be made by holding the prepared or lined cupcake tin at an angle and spooning the first coloured batter into the greased holes or paper cases. The second coloured batter is then spooned into the opposite side of the holes or paper cases, before baking.

Marbled cupcakes are made by gently swirling or lightly folding two different coloured batters together within each paper case before baking.

Filling cupcake cases/tin holes/silicone trays

🧁 When spooning the cupcake batter into the paper cases, cupcake holes or silicone trays, take care not to overfill them and divide the cupcake batter evenly between the cases/holes. They should be about two-thirds full. Use a dessertspoon and slide the batter off the spoon into each case with your little finger or another spoon. To fill mini muffin cases, use a teaspoon.

🧁 The amount of cupcake batter that you put into each cupcake case (or hole) will decide the size and shape of the baked cupcakes. If you fill the cases two-thirds full, these will bake into the traditional cupcake shape. If the cases are filled about half full, then the baked cupcakes will rise less inside the cases (up to or just below the top edge of the case) and will be smaller with a flatter top. If you fill the cases three-quarters full, then the baked cupcakes are likely to rise above the edge of the cases and expand outwards.

Common problems and solutions

🧁 Curdling – Curdling is the term used when the water from the eggs separates out from the fat globules in the cupcake mixture, and is usually caused by the eggs being too cold. A curdled cupcake mixture will hold less air and will produce cupcakes with a dense, flat texture. Also, if you add the eggs too quickly, the mixture will start to curdle. To help prevent curdling, use eggs at room temperature and add them gradually. If the creamed mixture does start to curdle, stir in a tablespoon or two of the measured flour to help bind the mixture back together, before adding more egg.

🧁 **Check you've put everything in** – Before you spoon the cupcake batter into the paper cases or prepared cupcake tin, make sure that you have incorporated all the ingredients required into the cupcake batter. If the batter isn't looking quite as you would expect it to, double check that nothing has been left out by mistake.

🧁 **Keeping things moving** – Don't leave the prepared cupcake batter hanging around. Once the cupcake batter is mixed, spoon it into the cupcake cases or holes, then immediately place the tin in the preheated oven. As soon as the wet and dry ingredients are combined, the raising agent will begin to work. So if the prepared cupcake batter is left to hang around at room temperature before baking, the leavening agents won't be as effective, the cupcakes won't rise as well and you'll end up with denser baked cupcakes.

If you have made a couple of tins of cupcakes, you are best to bake them all at the same time, if possible.

Chapter 3:
Bring On The Bake!

Checking the oven temperature

🧁 A reliable oven is essential to successful baking and it's a good idea to check yours regularly with an oven thermometer to make sure it's accurate.

🧁 A range of oven thermometers is available, most of which are stainless steel dial thermometers that hang or stand in the oven or clip onto the oven shelf. They vary in price, so choose one to suit your needs.

Where to place the cupcake tin

🧁 Unless otherwise stated, place your cupcake tin on the centre shelf of the oven to bake. With fan ovens, the temperature should be the same throughout the oven, but follow the manufacturer's instructions for specific guidelines.

🧁 Make sure your oven shelves/racks are level and make sure the tin does not touch the sides of the oven.

Checking the bake and testing for doneness

- Resist the temptation to keep opening the oven door to check on your cupcakes during baking. Don't be tempted to take a peek too soon, particularly early in the cooking time, as a sudden rush of cold air may cause the cupcakes to sink and the oven temperature will drop.

- To check if the cupcakes are ready, press the tops gently with your fingertip – the sponge should feel just firm and spring back without leaving an indentation.

- Another easy way to check the doneness of baked cupcakes is to insert a cocktail stick or a fine skewer into the centre of a cupcake. If it comes out clean, then the cupcakes are ready. If it's sticky and there is any uncooked cupcake batter or wetness on the cocktail stick, then the cupcakes are not quite ready and should be returned to the oven for a few more minutes to finish baking.

Cooling

- Once baked, leave the cupcakes to cool in the bun or muffin tin for 5–10 minutes to allow them to firm up a little. If you try to move them too quickly, they will crumble. Once they are cooled slightly, transfer the cupcakes to a wire cooling rack so that air can circulate and any excess steam can escape. This prevents condensation and allows the cupcakes to finish cooling quickly and evenly.

- If you don't have a wire cooling rack, use the rack from a grill pan or a barbecue rack.

- Allow the cupcakes to cool completely before icing or decorating. If you are storing them before decorating, always make sure your cupcakes are completely cool before storing, as any remaining steam may lead to condensation forming in the container, causing the cupcakes to go mouldy.

Storing

🧁 It almost goes without saying that a cupcake is best eaten on the day of making. However, you can store undecorated cupcakes in an airtight container for 2-3 days (make sure the baked cupcakes are completely cold before storing). Depending on the topping, decorated cupcakes will keep for 1-2 days in an airtight container.

🧁 It's best not to store cupcakes in the refrigerator unless they have a chocolate or cream-based topping. For any cupcakes with raw or lightly cooked egg whites in the frosting or topping, store in an airtight container in the refrigerator and eat within 2-3 days. Remove chilled cupcakes from the refrigerator about 30 minutes before serving.

🧁 Plain and buttercream-iced cupcakes can be frozen for up to 1 month. Use airtight containers or sealed polythene food bags for freezing.

Top tip

Cupcakes can be frozen for up to 1 month, but make sure they are thoroughly defrosted before eating.

Common cupcake baking problems and solutions

- **Over-peaked** – Too much raising agent in the batter or the oven temperature was too hot.

- **Dip in the centre** – Cupcakes were not cooked for long enough and/or the oven door was opened too soon.

- **Dense and heavy texture** – When making the cupcake batter, insufficient creaming or too heavy-handed when folding in.

- **Burnt bottoms** – Incorrect oven temperature used and oven was too hot. Or, the cupcake tin was placed directly on the oven floor (this is not advisable in some conventional electric ovens) instead of on an oven shelf.

- **Dry** – Most likely to be caused by over-baking or insufficient liquid added when making the batter. May also be due to cooling the cupcakes in a drafty atmosphere or storing them incorrectly.

- **Cupcakes rose unevenly** – Cupcake batter was not sufficiently mixed (i.e. flour and raising agent were not blended enough into the main mixture), or an uneven temperature inside the oven.

- **Top of cupcakes cracked** – Oven temperature was too hot so that the top crusts baked too quickly and the centre of the cupcakes continued to cook and rise, pushing through the top crusts and creating a cracked appearance.

Rescue remedies!

- If your baked cupcakes have burnt a little on top, scrape or thinly cut away the burnt bits with a serrated knife, then cover the tops with buttercream or frosting and decorate.

- If your baked cupcakes are too dry, try moistening them a little with a few drops or so of fresh orange or pineapple juice, light plain or flavoured sugar syrup, sweet sherry or a fruit liqueur, before decorating.

Chapter 4:
Let's Bling It Up!

Essential decorating equipment

🧁 For decorative piping of icings and frostings, you'll need piping bags and nozzles. Strong nylon or fabric bags are washable and reusable, while disposable polythene or paper bags save work. A small selection of stainless steel (or plastic) nozzles should include a plain writing nozzle, small and large star nozzles, and large plain nozzles.

🧁 Piping bags – These are easy to make from greaseproof or baking paper and can also be bought in paper, polythene or reusable nylon or fabric. Whether you choose to use reusable or disposable piping bags, make sure to suit the size of the bag to the quantity of frosting or icing you are using. Alternatively, make your own from greaseproof or baking paper (see page 29).

For piping cream, meringue, buttercream and other frostings, use large bags that allow plenty of room for filling. Don't over-fill the bag – you need to leave enough space at the top to twist it tightly closed to contain the frosting.

For royal or glacé icing, use a small or medium-sized bag. Disposable or paper piping bags are handy if you have a number of different coloured icings on the go at one time.

🧁 **Two-tone icing bags** – Specialist duo or split icing bags are also available and the dual compartment bag (which separates one icing from the other) allows you to pipe two different colours of icing or frosting at once through a nozzle (usually attached to a split coupler), giving you more scope for creativity. You can create your own simplified duo piping bag by spooning the two different coloured frostings each into a separate piping bag. Put both piping bags side by side into a larger piping bag fitted with a star-shaped nozzle, then pipe the frosting as required.

🧁 **Making a paper piping bag** – Take a 25-cm/10-inch square of greaseproof or baking paper. Fold it diagonally in half and cut into 2 triangles. Take 1 triangle and hold the 2 points at each end of the long edge. Curl 1 point over to meet the centre point making a cone shape, then curl the other point over so all 3 points meet. Fold the points over a few times to secure the cone. Snip off the end and use with or without a piping nozzle.

🧁 **Piping nozzles** – For piping buttercream, whipped cream or cream cheese frostings on top of cupcakes, you will need large metal or plastic nozzles with plain or star tips. Wide tips will allow the frosting to come out more quickly and produce big swirls.

For piping royal or glacé icing or more intricate decorations, use small metal nozzles with fine tips. You'll need one with a small plain tip for piping fine lines, dots, lettering and lacy patterns, and a star-tipped nozzle for piping shells, stars and rope patterns.

A coupler fitted to a piping bag is also useful to have as it allows you to change nozzles without emptying the bag.

- **Cutters** – Round plain or fluted cutters are ideal for stamping out rounds of fondant icing to top cupcakes. Small shaped cutters (hearts, numbers, flowers, letters, etc.) are great for simple but effective decorations.

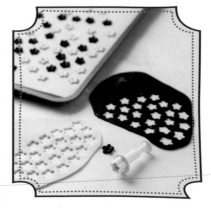

- **Rolling pin** – For rolling out small quantities of marzipan or fondant icing, it's worth buying a small non-stick rolling pin from a specialist cake decorating supplier.

- **Palette knives** – To swirl frosting onto cupcakes, you'll need a medium-sized palette knife. A small, angled palette knife is also useful for lifting and placing fondant icing shapes or other decorations onto the tops of cupcakes.

- **Pastry brush** – A good pastry brush is useful for brushing cupcakes with glaze before decorating. They are available with natural bristles or more durable synthetic bristles. Do make sure you clean pastry brushes thoroughly after use.

Basic frostings

- **Vanilla buttercream** – Smooth and buttery, vanilla buttercream frosting is the ideal topping for cupcakes. It's simple to make, keeps well and is easy to spread or pipe!

Makes enough to top 12 cupcakes
Preparation time: 10 minutes

150 g/5½ oz unsalted butter, softened
1 tsp vanilla extract
280 g/10 oz icing sugar
1–2 tbsp milk

Top tip

Palette knives are great for spreading buttercream thickly and evenly.

1. Place the butter and vanilla extract in a large mixing bowl and, using an electric mixer, beat the butter until very soft and pale.

2. Gradually sift in the icing sugar, beating well after each addition. The more you beat at this stage, the lighter and fluffier the frosting will be. Beat in the milk to give a softer consistency for piping.

If not using straightaway, transfer the buttercream to a small bowl and cover with clingfilm. It will keep in a cool place for 2–3 days. Stored in the refrigerator, buttercream will keep for up to a week but will become very firm, so leave at room temperature for at least 1 hour before using.

To colour, use a cocktail stick to add a tiny amount of food colouring paste or liquid to the buttercream. Beat thoroughly until you have an even colour.

Flavour variations for the basic vanilla buttercream recipe

- Chocolate – beat in 2 tablespoons of cocoa powder mixed to a paste with a little hot water, or 115 g/4 oz melted milk or plain chocolate.
- Lemon or orange – omit the milk and vanilla extract and beat in the finely grated rind and juice of 1 large lemon or orange.
- Coffee – replace the milk with 1-2 tablespoons of cold strong black brewed coffee or 1 tablespoon coffee and chicory essence.
- Caramel – beat in 1-2 tablespoons of dulce de leche (caramel sauce).

Cream cheese frosting – This is delicious used as a topping for carrot cupcakes as well as other flavoured cupcakes, including chocolate or vanilla. It is easy to spread and pipe and keeps for a few days in the refrigerator before use. Cupcakes decorated with this frosting are best eaten within 2 days.

Makes enough to top 12 cupcakes
Preparation time: 10 minutes

100 g/3½ oz full-fat cream cheese
50 g/1¾ oz unsalted butter, softened
1 tsp lemon juice
100 g/3½ oz icing sugar

1. Beat together the cream cheese and butter with an electric mixer until smooth.

2. Add the lemon juice and icing sugar and beat again until the frosting is creamy.

Basic icings

🧁 Royal icing – Royal icing is a smooth, fluid icing made from egg white and icing sugar. It's perfect for piping intricate decorations as it holds its shape well and sets hard. It's also useful for attaching decorations to fondant icing or for making pretty run-out designs to decorate cupcakes.

Makes about 165 g/5¾ oz
Preparation time: 10 minutes

2 tbsp egg white
150 g/5½ oz icing sugar, sifted
a few drops of lemon juice (optional)

1. Place the egg white in a bowl and, using a fork, whisk until just frothy.

2. Using an electric mixer or wooden spoon, gradually beat in the icing sugar until the mixture is stiff and stands up in peaks when the beaters or spoon are lifted. To get the desired consistency for piping, beat in a few drops of lemon juice.

A few drops of glycerine added with the lemon juice will stop the icing from setting too hard.

Once made, royal icing will keep for a few days (in a bowl or container) as long as the surface is closely covered with clingfilm. Beat thoroughly before using and add a few drops of warm water to loosen the icing if necessary.

Royal icing is best coloured with food colouring pastes as liquids will affect the piping consistency. Add colouring paste sparingly with a cocktail stick and beat well.

 Ready-to-roll fondant icing – Ready-to-roll fondant icing (also known as sugar paste) is a soft and pliable icing that is readily available. You'll find packs of white or ivory fondant icing in most supermarkets, and ready-coloured versions are available from specialist suppliers or online. Home-made ready-to-roll icing keeps for up to a week in a cool place, but must be thoroughly wrapped in clingfilm to prevent a crust forming. Lightly knead before use.

Makes 700 g/1 lb 9 oz
Preparation time: 15 minutes

1 egg white
2 tbsp liquid glucose
approx 625 g/1 lb 6 oz icing sugar

1. Put the egg white, glucose and 100 g/3½ oz of the icing sugar in a large bowl and mix with an electric mixer or a wooden spoon until smooth.

2. Work in more icing sugar until the paste becomes too stiff to mix. Turn out onto a surface dusted with icing sugar and gradually knead in more icing sugar with your hands until you have a smooth, very firm paste. If it's too soft, the icing will be sticky and difficult to roll out. Wrap thoroughly in clingfilm until ready to use.

Colouring fondant icing – It's best to use a food colouring paste to colour fondant icing as liquid will make it sticky. First, dust the work surface with icing sugar and knead the icing lightly until smooth and softened. Smear a little food colouring from the end of a cocktail stick onto the icing, then knead the icing until you have an even colour. Add a little more colouring until you get the desired depth of colour. Wrap the icing tightly in clingfilm to prevent it from drying out.

To marble fondant icing, knead 2 different colours of fondant icing lightly together. To achieve the best effect, use about one third of a deeply coloured icing and two thirds of a much paler colour or white icing and take care not to over-knead.

Glacé icing – Glacé icing is simply made from icing sugar and water. It gives a lovely smooth finish to cupcakes and sets softly in about 30 minutes. It's easy to flavour and colour and can be used to create pretty feathering or fanning effects or can be simply drizzled over cupcakes.

Makes enough to top 12 cupcakes
Preparation time: 5 minutes

175 g/6 oz icing sugar
5-6 tsp warm water

1. Sift the icing sugar into a bowl. Add 2 teaspoons of the warm water and beat well
    with a wooden spoon.

2. Continue adding the water, a little at a time, until you have a smooth and thick
    icing that will coat the back of the wooden spoon. Use immediately or cover the
    surface of the icing with clingfilm and use within 1 hour. Stir thoroughly before
    using and, if the icing has thickened a little, beat in a few drops of hot water.

To colour glacé icing, add a few drops of liquid food colouring or a very tiny amount
of colouring paste on the tip of a cocktail stick and stir until thoroughly mixed.

Flavour variations for the basic glacé icing recipe

*   Lemon or orange – replace the water with lemon or orange juice and add a little
    finely grated rind, if liked.
*   Coffee – replace the water with coffee essence or cold strong black coffee.
*   Chocolate – replace 25 g/1 oz of the icing sugar with cocoa powder.
*   Vanilla or almond – replace ½ teaspoon of the water with ½ teaspoon of vanilla
    or almond extract.

Using chocolate and decorating with chocolate

Melting chocolate – Chocolate can be melted on the hob or in the microwave. Both
methods work well, although you are better
able to control the heating temperature of
chocolate melted on the hob, particularly
milk and white chocolate which scorch easily
if over-heated.

To melt chocolate on the hob, break the
chocolate into pieces and place in a large
heatproof bowl. Set the bowl over a pan of
simmering water, making sure the bowl does
not touch the water underneath, and leave
until the chocolate has melted. Remove the
bowl from the pan and stir until smooth.

To melt chocolate in the microwave, break the pieces into a bowl and microwave for 1-2 minutes at a time on a Medium setting until almost completely melted. Remove from the microwave and leave to stand for 2 minutes, then stir until smooth. If there are any lumps remaining, microwave for another 30 seconds-1 minute.

Chocolate ganache – Luxurious chocolate ganache is the ultimate chocolate icing for cupcakes. Made from good-quality plain chocolate and double cream, it has a beautifully glossy sheen and is ideal for piping in large swirls on top of cupcakes.

Top tip

Chocolate can easily separate when it is melted so keep the heat as low as possible.

Makes enough to top 12 cupcakes
Preparation time: 10 minutes

150 g/5½ oz plain chocolate
200 ml/7 fl oz double cream

1. Finely chop the chocolate and place in a heatproof bowl. Heat the cream in a small saucepan until almost at boiling point. Pour the cream over the chocolate.

2. Stir until the chocolate has melted and the mixture is smooth and glossy.

For a pouring glaze to cover the tops of cupcakes, use immediately. For spreading, allow the ganache to cool for 15–20 minutes, stirring occasionally, until thickened.

For a firmer piping consistency, leave to cool for 5 minutes, then beat with an electric mixer until the ganache has cooled and thickened and is the consistency of softened butter.

To make small truffles to decorate cupcakes, chill the cooled ganache until firm. Roll into tiny balls and dust with cocoa powder or icing sugar.

🧁 Making chocolate caraque – Spread melted plain, milk or white chocolate in a thin and even layer onto a flat marble slab or a clean smooth surface. Leave until just set but not completely solid. Drag a thin-bladed sharp knife or scraper across the surface of the chocolate to scrape away long or short curls. If the chocolate breaks rather than curls, it is too cold. If it sticks to the knife, it has not set enough.

🧁 Making simple chocolate curls or shavings – Leave a chunky bar of chocolate at room temperature for at least an hour to soften a little. Run a swivel-headed vegetable peeler along the side of the bar of chocolate to shave off small curls or fine shavings. The curls can be made thicker by angling the peeler to get thicker curls.

If the chocolate is so cold that it breaks off in brittle pieces, warm very briefly for a few seconds in the microwave.

🧁 Making chocolate leaves – Fresh leaves with well defined veins, such as bay, rose, mint and holly, are best to use. Make sure they are thoroughly clean and dry. Brush the underside of each leaf thickly with melted chocolate, taking care not to let the chocolate go over the edges of the leaves. If you are using holly leaves, don't let the chocolate drip over the prickly points. Place the leaves chocolate-side up on a sheet of baking paper and leave in a cool place until set. Carefully peel away the leaves from the chocolate. It's worth making more than you need as they are quite fragile.

🧁 **Making piped chocolate shapes** – Line a tray with baking paper. Spoon melted chocolate into a paper piping bag and snip off the very end tip of the bag. Pipe simple shapes, such as flowers, swirls or motifs, onto the paper. Don't make them too intricate or they will be too fragile. Leave in a cool place until set, then carefully peel the paper away from the chocolate. Use a small palette knife to move the shapes as the warmth of your fingers will melt the finely piped chocolate.

Rolling, cutting out and moulding fondant icing

🧁 **Rolling out fondant icing** – Lightly dust a clean work surface with icing sugar and knead the icing until smooth. Using a small rolling pin (a non-stick one is best), roll out thinly, lifting and turning the icing occasionally to prevent it from sticking.

🧁 **Cutting out shapes** – To top cupcakes with a round of fondant icing, use a round or fluted cutter that is roughly the size of the top of the cupcake. Stamp the cutter firmly onto the rolled-out icing, twisting it slightly. Brush or spread a little jam, chocolate spread, glacé icing or royal icing on the top of the cupcake. Lift the round of fondant icing with a palette knife and gently place on top of the cupcake.

For small shapes, such as stars, hearts, letters, numbers and flowers, roll out a small amount of fondant icing. Stamp out the required shapes and carefully lift with a small angled palette knife. To attach the shapes to fondant-topped cupcakes, use a dab of water, glacé icing or royal icing to stick them into place.

To dry small shapes for decoration, place on a sheet of baking paper and leave in a cool place for at least 24 hours. Once firm, they can be placed at angles on top of frosted cupcakes.

Alternatively, cut out small shapes, such as stars or hearts, and then push a cocktail stick into the base of each one and place on a sheet of baking paper to harden. An icing shape on a cocktail stick can then be inserted into the top of each iced cupcake to decorate, just before serving.

🧁 **Moulding shapes** – Using small pieces of fondant icing you can mould simple shapes to decorate cupcakes. Lightly dust your hands with icing sugar to prevent the icing from sticking to them.

Decorating with marzipan and creating marzipan or fondant roses and flower shapes

🧁 **Decorating with marzipan** – This pliable almond paste can be used in the same way as fondant icing to decorate cupcakes, but it has a slightly moister texture, which makes it a bit trickier to colour and roll out thinly.

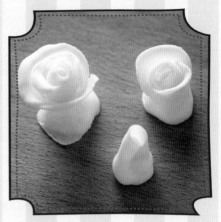

When colouring marzipan, use the white variety and take care not to add too much colouring as it will become sticky.

🧁 **Making marzipan or fondant roses** – Roll 6 or 7 pea-sized pieces of marzipan or ready-to-roll fondant icing in the palm of your hand into balls. Place the balls between 2 sheets of clingfilm and flatten with a small rolling pin to make petal shapes.

Place a marble-sized piece of marzipan or fondant icing on a small board and shape into a pointed cone for the base of the rose. Take 1 of the petals and gently wrap around the cone base to form a bud.

Continue wrapping the petals around the bud to create a rose, squeezing the base of the rose gently to make the petals curl out (dust your fingers lightly with icing sugar if the marzipan or icing becomes sticky). Use a sharp knife to cut the rose away from the base, place on a baking sheet lined with baking paper and leave to dry in a cool place.

To dust the edges with edible glitter, use a fine paintbrush to lightly brush the tops of the petals with a little water. Dip the roses into edible glitter, then gently tap the roses on a sheet of kitchen paper to remove any excess glitter. Leave in a cool place, uncovered, until hardened and dry.

Make as many roses as you need in the same way, varying the sizes of the cones and petals to make small and large roses, if liked.

🧁 **Creating fondant or marzipan flower shapes** – Line a baking sheet with baking paper. Roll out ready-to-roll fondant icing or marzipan thinly on a surface very lightly dusted with icing sugar.

Press a 1-cm/½-inch flower plunger cutter into the icing or marzipan. Lift away the cutter and transfer the icing shapes to the prepared baking sheet, pressing out the shape with the plunger.

Press the flowers onto a buttercream-topped cupcake and then pipe a small dot into the centre of each flower.

The flowers can be shaped well in advance. Once hardened, store them in an airtight container between layers of kitchen paper for up to 2 weeks.

Piping frostings and icings

When piping frostings and icings, different shaped nozzles will produce varied looks, so get creative and experiment to see what looks most appealing!

🧁 Piping buttercream and frosting – Piping buttercream onto cupcakes gives a professional finish and is surprisingly easy.

To fill a piping bag with buttercream or frosting, use a large piping bag fitted with a star or plain nozzle. Hold the piping bag in one hand with the top of the bag folded down over your fingers and thumb. Use a spatula to scoop the frosting into the bag. Unfold the top of the bag, then gently smooth the frosting down into the bag to remove any pockets of air. Twist the bag tightly at the top to prevent the frosting from being squeezed up and out of the bag.

Alternatively, you can place the piping bag in a tall glass and fold the top of the bag over the rim of the glass. This will leave you with both hands free to fill the bag with frosting and the glass will hold the bag steady.

To pipe swirls of buttercream or frosting, use a piping bag fitted with a large star nozzle and position the tip of the piping nozzle near the outer edge of the top of the cupcake. Squeeze the piping bag firmly and, as the frosting comes out of the nozzle, gently rotate the piping bag in a decreasing circle towards the centre of the cupcake. Once the top of the cupcake is covered, stop squeezing the bag and lift the nozzle gently away from the cupcake to give a pointed peak of frosting in the centre.

For large swirls of buttercream or frosting, pipe 2 or 3 decreasing circles of frosting on top of the cupcake, gently lifting the bag as you go.

To pipe rose swirls of buttercream or frosting, use a medium-sized star nozzle and start piping from the centre of the cupcake. Keep the nozzle close to the top of the cupcake and continue piping in a spiral pattern until the cupcake is covered.

🧁 **Piping royal or glacé icing** – For lines and lettering, use a small piping bag fitted with a fine writing nozzle. Place the tip of the nozzle on the surface to be iced and squeeze the bag gently. As the icing comes out of the nozzle, lift the bag so the icing falls in a straight line or curve on the surface. To finish piping, stop squeezing and gently press the tip of the nozzle on the surface to neatly end the line of icing. Leave to set.

🧁 **Cornelli lace effect** – Use a small piping bag fitted with a fine writing nozzle. Starting at an outer edge, pipe a random meandering continuous line of icing all over the surface of the cupcake. Try not to let the lines touch or cross and keep even pressure on the piping bag so the lines are of the same thickness. Leave to set.

Frosting by hand

The simplest way to top cupcakes with buttercream is to spread or swirl the frosting with a palette knife. Here's a quick guide to a variety of different finishes. First, make sure that the buttercream is as smooth and creamy as possible with no small lumps by beating thoroughly with a spatula.

For a simple lightly swirled topping, take a good scoop of buttercream on the palette knife and place it on the top of the cupcake. Spread the frosting to the edges of the cupcake and, using a to-and-fro motion and without lifting the palette knife from the frosting, spread the buttercream evenly over the cake.

To create a smooth domed effect, perfect for coating with sugar sprinkles, add more buttercream to the centre of the cupcake. Use the palette knife to smooth the frosting right down to the edge of the cupcake case, then lightly smooth the top.

To achieve a raised edge effect, add a little more buttercream and spread it out to the edges of the cupcake leaving a small dip in the middle. Holding the palette knife at an angle to the side of the cupcake, drag it all around the cupcake to give a smooth raised edge of frosting.

For a really generously topped cupcake with big swirls of frosting, add another scoop of buttercream to the top of the cupcake. Drag the end of the palette knife through the frosting in the centre of the cupcake in a circular motion to create a deep swirl. Without lifting the palette knife from the frosting, drag it back in the opposite direction, then quickly lift the palette knife away.

Feather icing and fan icing

To feather-ice cupcakes, spoon glacé icing over the top of the cupcakes to cover completely. Spoon contrasting coloured or flavoured glacé icing into a piping bag fitted with a fine nozzle and quickly pipe parallel lines across the top. Use a cocktail stick to draw lightly across the piped lines in alternate directions to create a feathered effect.

To fan-ice cupcakes, instead of piping lines of contrasting icing, pipe 3 or 4 concentric circles. Create a fanned or spider's web effect by alternately drawing a cocktail stick through the icing from the centre of the cupcake to the edge and from the edge back to the centre.

Writing icing and edible ink marker pens

🧁 Tubes of different coloured writing icing are readily available, including chocolate icing tubes, and can be used as a quick and easy way to decorate cupcakes.

🧁 Edible ink markers or cake decorating pens are also useful for drawing designs or features on edible gum paste, fondant or other sugar icing decorations. Edible paint and food colouring sprays in a range of colours are also available from specialist suppliers.

Piping gel and edible gum paste

🧁 Clear piping gel can be left clear or coloured with food colouring and used to decorate cupcakes. It is also handy for attaching edible gum paste decorations or other decorations or sprinkles. Tubes of coloured decorating gels are also available and are ideal for writing or drawing patterns on your cupcakes to add eye-catching detail and colour.

🧁 Ready-to-use edible gum paste or modelling paste is handy for moulding and creating flowers and other decorations for your cupcakes.

Adding sprinkles, glitter and decorations

🧁 Sugar sprinkles – The simplest and easiest way to give frosted or iced cupcakes a touch of colourful fun, sugar sprinkles are readily available in a huge variety of colours, shapes and sizes. From classic coloured sugars and hundreds and thousands to small shimmering pearls, pastel-coloured flower shapes or tiny red hearts or multi-coloured stars, there's a sprinkle to suit any occasion! Always add sprinkles before the icing or frosting has set, otherwise they will drop off.

🧁 Sanding or glimmering sugar – These are coarse sugars with grains about 4 times larger than granulated sugar that won't dissolve. You can buy them in a range of pastel or vibrant colours. They add a stylish sparkle, as well as some crunch, when sprinkled over iced cupcakes.

Edible glitter – Available in tiny pots from cake decorating or specialist suppliers, a little edible glitter can really add the finishing touch to cupcakes for special occasions. Lightly sprinkle over an iced cupcake or use a fine paint brush to brush onto fondant icing or piped decorations. Use sparingly.

Lustre spray – Available in a variety of colours from specialist suppliers, lustre spray adds elegance and style to cupcakes with its appealing sheen. Edible silk or lustre food dust or powder is also available in several colours and can be used as an alternative to edible glitter.

- ☕ **Candy melts** – Available from specialist suppliers, these are versatile coloured sweet candy coatings that can be used for making decorations or decorating. The candy melts are melted, poured or piped and left to set before using/serving.

- ☕ **Sweets and chocolates** – Small sweets and chocolates are great for jazzing up frosted cupcakes. Chocolate buttons, jelly beans, sugar-coated chocolates and candy bears are all ideal for children's party cupcakes, and a sprinkling of popping candy just before serving will make them extra special and add a tongue-tingling surprise!

- ☕ **Sugar flowers and shapes** – Simple sugar flowers, fondant animal shapes or themed seasonal shapes are ideal to have in the storecupboard for last-minute decorations.

- ☕ **Fresh fruit** – For a refreshing and delicious alternative to sweet sugary sprinkles, use fresh fruit to decorate cupcakes. Try grapes, small summer berries or slices of mango, pineapple, peach or apricot. Arrange on the frosting or icing just before serving and eat on the day of topping.

Top tip

Dragées in a contrasting colour create a stunning effect on frosted cupcakes.

🧁 **Crystallized rose petals or violets** – Delicately perfumed and with a crisp sugary coating, a single deep pink rose petal or purple violet will look stunning on top of a simply iced cupcake.

🧁 **Nuts** – Finely chopped, toasted, whole, halved or flaked, nuts are a quick and easy way to decorate a cupcake and can complement a flavouring or frosting. To lightly toast nuts, spread on a baking sheet and place in a hot oven for a few minutes until light golden or pop under a hot grill. Cool completely before use.

🧁 **Coconut** – Desiccated, flaked or shredded coconut is another quick and effective decoration for cupcakes. Use lightly toasted for an extra nutty flavour.

🧁 **Dragées** – These tiny and shiny edible balls are classic cupcake decorations. They are available in a variety of shimmering colours, including silver, gold, pink, blue and green. You can also buy large silver balls or heart-shaped dragées.

- **Fresh flowers and herbs** – For a lovely summery decoration, try topping cupcakes with fresh flowers. Make absolutely sure that the flowers are edible (see page 55 for examples of edible flowers) and wash them carefully in cold water, then leave to dry on kitchen paper in a cool place before using. Place either the whole flower or a few petals on the cupcake just before serving. Herbs, such as mint and lemon balm, also make pretty decorations, especially when used with fresh or sugar-frosted fruit.

- **Candied citrus peel** – With a firm and slightly grainy texture, candied lemon, orange or citron peel can be chopped or cut into thin strips to decorate iced cupcakes. For a more striking decoration, dip very thin strips of peel in melted plain chocolate and leave to set on a wire cooling rack, then arrange a few strips on each cupcake.

- **Edible cupcake toppers** – To add a special finishing touch to cupcakes, a wide range of edible cake toppers is available to suit all occasions and age groups, including novelty shapes, animal shapes, decorative figures and themed toppers. They are obtainable in a variety of types, including sugar or sugarcraft shapes, chocolate shapes or edible wafer/rice paper shapes.

🧁 **Non-edible decorations** – Cake candles and indoor sparklers make great last-minute decorations, especially for birthday or special occasion cupcakes. Cake candles are available as standard candles (such as striped, spotty or glitter party candles, with plastic candle holders) or as novelty-shaped candles attached to sticks, including butterflies, flowers, letters, hearts, stars, mini cupcakes and many more.

Colour co-ordinate candles with icing or frosting, sugar sprinkles and cupcake cases for an impressive effect.

Small plastic figurines or shapes can also be used to suit an occasion, but do remind everyone they are not edible and must be removed before eating the cupcakes.

Adding flavour to cupcakes

🧁 Brushing or spooning syrup over cupcakes while they are still warm from the oven will infuse them with extra flavour, as well as helping to keep them deliciously moist. This is especially useful when making a big batch of cupcakes for a special event.

🧁 To make a basic sugar syrup, place 40 g/1½ oz caster sugar and 4 tablespoons of water in a small pan and heat gently until the sugar dissolves. Boil, without stirring, for about 1 minute, until syrupy, then leave to cool for at least 10 minutes.

🧁 Use a skewer to pierce a few holes in the top of the warm cupcakes and liberally spoon or brush the syrup over the top. Leave to cool completely before topping with frosting or icing.

Syrup flavours

- Lemon or orange – replace the water with lemon or orange juice.
- Coffee – add 2 teaspoons of instant coffee granules.
- Rum – replace 2 tablespoons of the water with dark rum.
- Vanilla or almond – add 1 teaspoon of vanilla or almond extract.

Hidden fillings for cupcakes after baking

🧁 To add a surprise element to baked cupcakes, try scooping out a little of the sponge and adding a sweet filling.

🧁 Suit the filling to the flavour of the cupcake. Strawberry or raspberry jam goes particularly well with vanilla or almond cupcakes. Try chocolate spread with chocolate or coffee cupcakes and lemon curd or marmalade with citrus-flavoured cupcakes.

🧁 To scoop out the sponge, make sure the cupcake is completely cold then use a teaspoon or the tip of a small knife to cut away a small piece of sponge. Spoon a little of the filling into the hole, taking care not to over-fill, and then place the piece of sponge back in place, pressing down gently.

🧁 Another way to add a surprise filling to baked cupcakes is to use an apple corer or a specialist cupcake corer/plunger to remove the centre of each cupcake. The centres can then be filled (with buttercream, jam, chocolate spread, fruit purée, etc.) before topping the cupcakes with frosting and decorating them.

Coating and edging cupcakes

🧁 A simple way to give frosted cupcakes a colourful or decorative finish is to coat the top or edges lightly with sugar sprinkles, grated chocolate, finely chopped nuts, coloured sugar or crushed boiled sweets.

🧁 To edge cupcakes, spread the coating on a flat plate. Hold a cupcake by its base and quickly roll the raised frosted edge in the coating, shaking off any excess.

🧁 To completely coat cupcakes, smooth frosting over the cupcake in a raised mound. Hold the cupcake over a plate and liberally sprinkle with the coating, pressing down lightly with your fingers if necessary.

🧁 When using buttercream, it's best to frost and coat the cupcakes one at a time, otherwise the frosting will dry a little and the coating will not stick.

Stencilling designs and patterns on cupcakes

🧁 Simple but very effective designs and patterns can be created for the tops of cupcakes using bought or home-made stencils and a dusting of cocoa powder, icing sugar, coloured sugar, finely grated chocolate or edible silk or lustre food dust or powder.

🧁 Small coffee stencils with simple designs, such as hearts, flowers and stars, are ideal to use. Hold steadily close to the surface of the cupcake and liberally spoon or shake over sifted cocoa powder, icing sugar, coloured sugar or sprinkles. Carefully lift away the stencil.

🧁 Alternatively, cut out your own simple shapes (such as a heart, star, etc.) from a piece of card or thick paper or, to create a lacy pattern, cut a round piece of a paper doily to fit the top of the cupcake.

🧁 For a geometric design or a lattice effect, lay thin strips of paper gently on top of the cupcake at intervals and dust liberally with icing sugar or cocoa powder. Very carefully lift away the strips of paper.

Sugar frosting

- Choose firm fresh berries, such as blueberries, raspberries, redcurrants and strawberries, or small grapes. Make sure that they have no blemishes or soft patches.

- Flowers or single petals should be clean and edible. Rose petals work especially well, but other edible flowers include lavender, marigolds, pansies and nasturtiums.

- Leafy fresh herbs, such as mint, lemon balm and bay, are ideal for sugar frosting, or try small sprigs of fresh thyme or marjoram.

- Using a small paintbrush, lightly brush the fruit, flowers, petals or leaves all over with a little beaten egg white, making sure to coat the underside of leaves and petals.

- Coat flowers with sugar by holding over a plate and sprinkling liberally with caster sugar, shaking off any excess sugar. To coat leaves, petals and berries, place the sugar on a flat plate and either dip or roll in the sugar to coat.

- Place on a sheet of baking paper or a wire cooling rack and leave in a cool place for a few hours or overnight until dry. Soft berry fruits will only keep for a day, but grapes, leaves and flowers will keep for 2–3 days if stored in a cool, dry place.

Chapter 5:
Serving With Style!

Top tip

A tiered cupcake stand is a gorgeous way to display decorated cupcakes.

Perfect presentation

Whether you've just got friends over for a coffee or you're celebrating a more formal occasion, such as a birthday or wedding, make your home-made cupcakes centre stage by arranging them on pretty plates or stands.

- **Cupcake wrappers or wraps** – These decorative strips of light card come in a variety of patterns and colours and are great for wrapping around individual cupcakes. They enhance decorated cupcakes and add style and appeal. Some have themed or patterned designs while others have laced or scalloped edges. They are simply wrapped around single cupcakes and sealed with a tab fastening.

- **Cake plates** – Elegantly decorated cupcakes look even more delicious when arranged on pretty tea plates or saucers or china cake stands. Make sure that you don't position the cupcakes too close together – allow enough room so that you can take a cake from the plate or stand without damaging any of the others. Add extra decorations around the cupcakes, if you like, such as small flowers, fresh herbs, sugared almonds, ribbons or small bows.

- **Cupcake stands** – These are ideal for displaying and serving lots of cupcakes. Special metal stands (sometimes called cupcake tree stands) with individual wired holders or baskets for each cupcake, which ensure that the frosting or icing doesn't get damaged, are ideal. Alternatively, look out for affordable, flat-packed, disposable cardboard cupcake stands in a variety of colours and patterns, including themed designs. These are practical and easy to assemble as the sections simply slot together. Both types can usually hold between 20–30 cupcakes – enough for a party or small wedding. For a larger quantity of cupcakes, it may be worth hiring a tiered cake stand from a specialist cake supplier or make your own tiered stand using different-sized cake boards and cake pillars.

To add a sophisticated look to your cupcakes or to dress up a table for afternoon tea, individual or miniature cupcake stands or pedestals are also obtainable from specialist suppliers. These attractive plain or patterned cardboard cupcake stands (petal-shaped, teapot shapes, etc.) or rigid clear plastic pedestals are easy to assemble at home.

- **Gift boxes** – Available in a huge range of sizes, colours and designs, gift boxes are an ideal way to give cupcakes as presents. Look for boxes with a clear panel in the top so that you can see the contents without opening the lid, or choose clear plastic boxes. Luxury gift boxes are also obtainable. Good kitchenware stores or specialist suppliers stock cupcake boxes with special inserts into which you can slot the cupcakes to hold them safely in place. Most gift boxes hold several cupcakes (usually 4, 6 or 12, or sometimes more), but single cupcake gift boxes are also obtainable. Tie pretty ribbons or raffia around the boxes to add a special finishing touch.

🧁 **Cellophane bags** – These are the perfect way to present a single cupcake as a gift. They are available in clear or patterned versions. Tie them with a pretty ribbon or some raffia for an extra special touch. Rigid clear plastic individual (or twin) dome pods, with hinged lids, are also available as an alternative.

🧁 **Cake stands** – For simple but effective presentation, proudly display your cupcakes on a standard cake stand. Cake stands vary in shape and design and include round, square, ornate or simple stands, short or tall pedestal stands, or dome or covered stands, so choose one that suits your style and the occasion.

🧁 **Cake boards or platters** – Foil- or paper-covered cake boards are suitable for displaying cupcakes and, depending on the type of presentation you are looking for, cake platters or trays can also be used.

🧁 **Decorated boxes or baskets** – Transform your cupcakes into something special by displaying them in decorative boxes or lined wicker baskets, finished with colour-matching ribbons or raffia.

🧁 **Cupcake flags or sticks picks** – Available in different designs, these decorative flags can add an individual touch to decorated cupcakes. Most are double-sided. Alternatively, create your own designs using cocktail sticks and plain or coloured paper or thin card.

Creating a display for a special occasion

🧁 A stunning display of cupcakes on a table can replace a large, iced cake for a special occasion, creating an impressive centrepiece for many celebrations, including birthdays, christenings, anniversaries and weddings.

🧁 Try to select a tablecloth, or varying layers of tablecloth, that complements the colour of the cupcakes or their paper cases. You could also place some attractively decorated or coloured napkins on the table display as well, to add a variety of colour and patterns. Some coloured ribbon or table runners draped over the table will also create a beautiful effect.

🧁 Use different-sized plastic or cardboard boxes placed underneath the tablecloth to create flat platforms at various levels, onto which you can then place your plates or stands of cupcakes.

🧁 A tiered cupcake stand or cupcake tree stand can really show off chic cupcake creations with style. Cupcake stands can create a spectacular display and come in many designs and styles that are a work of art in themselves. Silver or colour-finished metal stands are great for weddings, while brightly coloured cardboard stands may be better for a children's birthday party.

🧁 As well as practical items, such as serving plates and paper napkins for guests, you could also add a few decorative items to the table to finish off the display (depending on your theme), such as candlesticks, vases, posies of fresh or dried flowers, and so on. You could try draping a colour contrasting or matching piece of fabric or some bunting behind the table as a chic backdrop. You could also place a few bunches of fresh or dried herbs on the table or add some colourful streamers or confetti shapes.

Holding a cupcake decorating party

Indulge in some cupcake fun and host a cupcake decorating party for children or adults. As part of the party entertainment, everyone can have some fantastic fun, get creative and get involved in icing and decorating cupcakes.

🧁 Cupcake decorating parties are suitable for many occasions, including children's birthday parties (suitable for many age groups), toddler and children's groups, or teenage get-togethers or sleepovers. Cupcake parties geared towards adults could include birthday parties, hen parties, a girls' night in or just a gathering of a group of friends. Children and adults alike will love getting involved and are sure to enjoy creating their own appealing cupcakes, so tailor the party to suit your guests.

🧁 Provide your guests with a selection of freshly baked cold cupcakes ready for decorating. Arrange containers or bowls of a choice of frostings and icings and a selection of fun toppings (including sweets, glitters, sparkles and toppers) for guests to choose from – they can then decorate the cupcakes in their own style and design, to suit their taste preferences.

🧁 It's a good idea to provide aprons for your guests (and hats too, if you like!), especially for children's parties, and don't forget to supply spoons, spatulas, palette knives and basic piping equipment for spreading or piping frostings and icings.

 You could supply gift boxes so that your guests can take home their decorated cupcakes (if they don't all get eaten at the party!). You could also demonstrate some basic decorating styles to give your guests some ideas before they begin.

Hosting a cupcake party

If you want an excuse to get together with family for a special occasion, to invite colleagues over for a fund-raising event, or to simply spend time with friends catching up on gossip one afternoon, you can host a cupcake party!

Make, bake, decorate and display all the cupcakes before your guests arrive and they can then tuck straight into your tasty delights. Serve the cupcakes with a refreshing glass of something nice and enjoy the time spent together.

You could create a themed cupcake party if you like and display your baked goodies in various ways (see page 58) to add extra appeal and delight. Remember to provide your guests with small plates or saucers and napkins to eat their cupcakes, and offer forks if the cupcakes are likely to be a little trickier to eat!

Transporting cupcakes to a venue

If you are not hosting the party at your home, you'll need to carefully transport your cupcakes to the chosen venue.

🧁 If you are hosting a cupcake party at a venue other than your home and you have limited time, transport the cupcakes in a decorated state. Otherwise, pack undecorated, cold baked cupcakes and take the frostings and toppings in separate containers, then decorate and display the cupcakes at the venue before the party.

🧁 If you are tight for time at the venue, then large, shallow plastic containers are ideal for transporting decorated cupcakes as they can be stored in a single layer.

Purpose-made cupcake boxes or carriers comprising a rectangular plastic latched container that holds several stackable plastic cupcake trays inside (each 12-hole tray holds cupcakes securely in place), with a carrying handle on top, are ideal for transporting cupcakes to events and parties and are good for storage too.

Cupcake caddies are also obtainable and these hold standard or mini cupcakes in a single (reversible) tray, within a latched base and see-through cover with carrying handle.

These are all available from good kitchenware stores, specialist suppliers, catering suppliers or online.

🧁 Another way to prevent iced and decorated cupcakes moving around as you transport them to a party is to place them back into a clean cupcake baking tin. Loosely cover the tin and cupcakes with foil or clingfilm (taking care not to disturb the decorated tops).

Once you arrive at the venue, the cupcakes can then be carefully removed from the tin and transferred to a platter, plates, tray or cupcake stand for serving.

Index